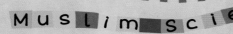

# IBN YUNUS
## The Father of Astronomy

Published by Ali Gator Productions
Copyright © 2017 Ali Gator Productions, First Edition,
First Published 2017

National Library of Australia Cataloguing–in-Publication (CIP) data:
Ahmed Imam
ISBN: 978-1-921772-37-5
For primary school age, Juvenile fiction, Dewey Number: 823.92

Adopted from the original title Ilmuan Muslim Ibnu Yunus first published by Pelangi Mizan.
Copyright © 2015 by Author Risma Dewi, Illustrator Nano. Printed in Indonesia.

T: +61 (3) 9386 2771  F: +61 (3) 9478 8854
P.O. Box 2536, Regent West, Melbourne Victoria, 3072 Australia
E: info@ali-gator.com  W: www.ali-gator.com

بِسْمِ اللهِ الرَّحْمَٰنِ الرَّحِيمِ

*BISMILLAHIR RAHMANIR RAHIM*

IN THE NAME OF ALLAH, MOST GRACIOUS, MOST MERCIFUL

Inspiring our children to learn about
the great Muslim scientists, scholars
and adventurers from the
Golden Age of Islam.

# NOTES TO PARENTS AND TEACHERS

The Muslim Scientists Series aims to introduce to young readers some of the famous Muslim scientists, scholars and adventurers who discovered and invented many things that we use today and take for granted.

Whilst reading about Ibn Yunus, "The Father of Astronomy", talk to the children about the stars and the moon. Ask them about using a telescope to see the stars. Take them out at night and look at the stars together.
Did you know that there is a crater on the moon named after "Ibn Yunus". How amazing is that?

Make a pendulum and watch it move from side to side, and explain how clocks in the past were once like this.

In Sha Allah (God Willing) if this series helps to inspire our young readers to be the next generation of thinkers, to better mankind through inventions and discoveries, then we have truly met our goal.

Ibn Yunus was born in Egypt around the Year 950.

He is known as one of the greatest astronomers of Islam.
Some people called him "The Father of Astronomy,"
because of his great knowledge.

Astronomy is the study of the sun, moon,
stars, and the planets.

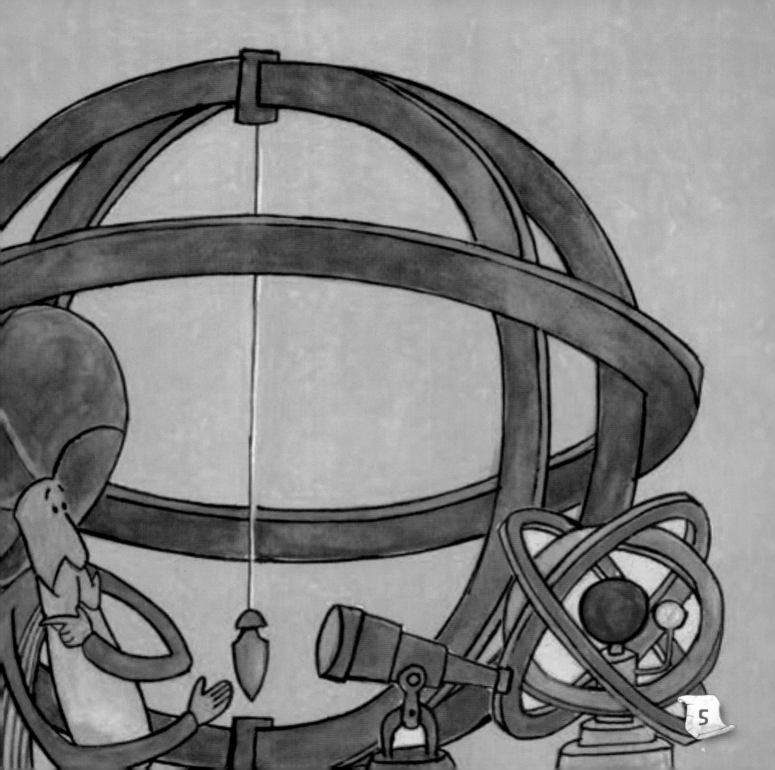

Ibn Yunus came from a very respected family.
His father, 'Abd al Rahman, was a famous historian
and scholar of Hadith (the sayings of Prophet
Muhammad PBUH) and known as
"The author of the History of Egypt".

*PBUH – PEACE BE UPON HIM*

From a young age Ibn Yunus was always looking at the stars and thinking about them.

In the Qur'an* it says:

الشَّمْسُ وَالْقَمَرُ بِحُسْبَانٍ

Ashamsu waal qamaru bihusbaan

"The sun and the moon (move)
by precise calculations"

How could this be thought Ibn Yunus ?

* Surah 55 Ar-Rahman –.Ayat 5

9

So when he was older Ibn Yunus studied to understand what Allah had said in the Qur'an.

He started to measure how the different planets moved around the sun using these large rings.

The rings were so big a horse could fit between them.

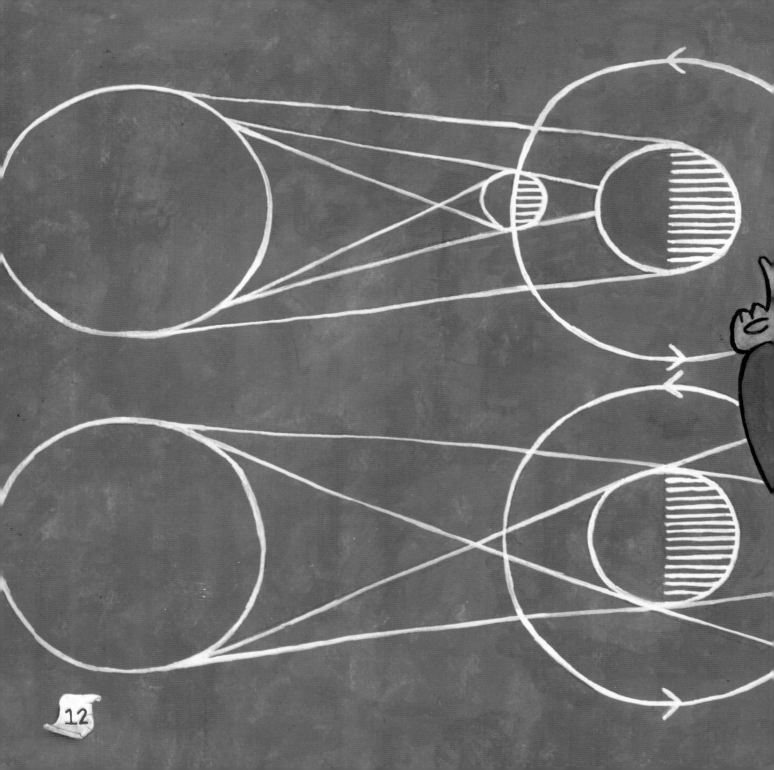

And then it happened. The breakthrough he was looking for.

Ibn Yunus calculated that there was going to be a solar eclipse.

This is when the moon goes in front of the sun, which turns the day into darkness.

When the eclipse happened on April 22nd, 981 Ibn Yunus became famous.

This was the first time a solar eclipse had ever been measured.

After this historical event Ibn Yunus was given permission to build an observatory in Cairo.

From here he could study the stars and all their movements.

15

For more than 30 years Ibn Yunus studied and measured the planets, the stars, the sun and the moon.

He recorded his findings in his famous book "Al Zij Hakimi Al Kabir" that scientists still use today.

16

His book of calculations were so accurate, it even described when eclipses would take place up to 250 years after his death.

From this book his reputation grew and grew.

17

Ibn Yunus also became the first person to use the sun and the moon to calculate the different Muslim prayer times for the different times of the year.

This incredible man also developed a way to calculate the Qibla, the direction Muslims pray, (towards the Kaaba) in Makkah, from anywhere in the world.

We owe a lot to the discoveries of Ibn Yunus.

Ibn Yunus became so famous for his observations of the stars, that there is now a crater on the moon named after him. The "Ibn Yunus" crater.

It can be seen from earth.

Do you know what this is ?
It's a Pendulum.

Ibn Yunus was also the first scientist
to measure the movement back and forth of
the pendulum.

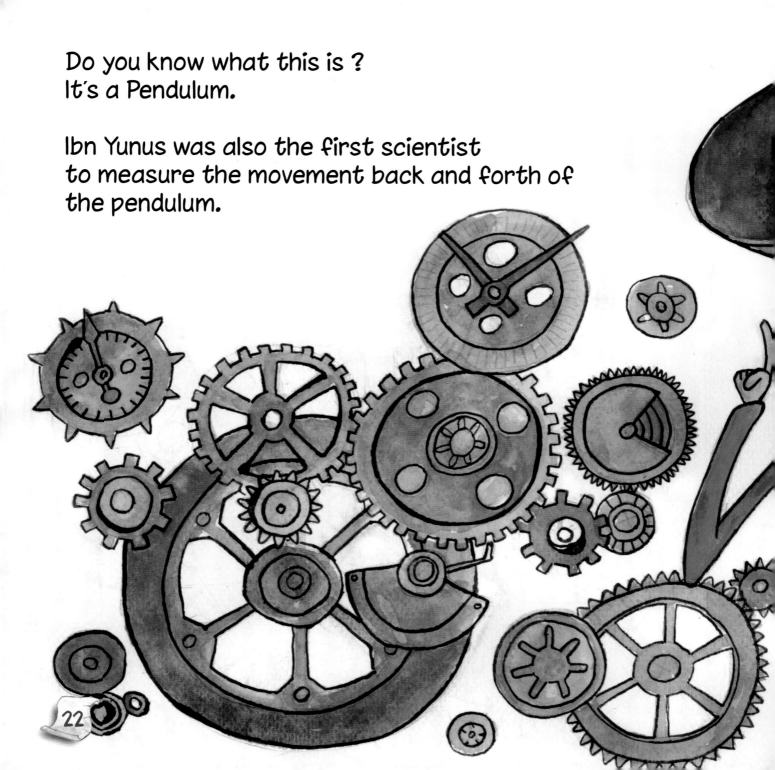

From this discovery later on clocks were invented to measure time.

Ibn Yunus was truly an amazing man.
Ma Sha Allah.

*MA SHA ALLAH* – ALLAH HAS WILLED IT

الْحَمْدُ لِلَّهِ

*ALHAMDULILLAH - PRAISE BE TO ALLAH*

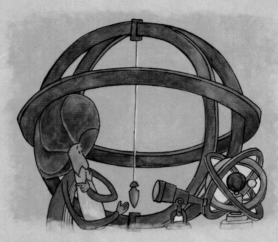

Every child should learn this Dua´ (supplication) to ask Allah to help increase them in knowledge and understanding.

رَبِّ زِدْنِي عِلْمًا

Rabbi Zidni ´ilman

"Oh Allah, Increase Me in Knowledge"

Qur´an Surah: 20 (Ta Ha) Verse: 114